grace
go bloom
PRINT MAGAZINE

GROW

Grace Go Bloom is a quarterly print magazine for Christians in the creative industries. We aim to encourage faith, provide business-building workshops, spark fresh creative ideas and develop a sense of community among artists of all specialties in God's world-wide church.

ISBN978-1-7751875-8-5 (Print)

www.gracegobloom.com

Contributors

Photography (listed per article)

EDITOR IN CHIEF
Eleanor Krause

THIS IS GRACE GO BLOOM
Adrien Olichon

ART DIRECTION
Lottie Aldarwish

GOD CAN USE US JUST THE WAY WE ARE
Daniele Levis Pelusi

Micheile dot com

Evie S

Mathew Schwartz

DEVOTIONAL
Jessica Rupp

GOD CAN USE US JUST THE WAY WE ARE
Margaret Ramage

GROWING PAINS
Yusuf Evli

Matthew Henry

Hello I'm Nik

GROW FROM HERE
Caitlin Forster

GROWING PAINS
Esther Karram

LYRICS
Freestocks.org

POEM
Demi Cheryl

REFINED BY FIRE
Mulyadi

Esteban Amaro

Drew Beamer

NURTURING CREATIVITY
Betsey Iannarelli

REFINED BY FIRE
Michelle Perkett

FINDING VALUE
Milad Fakurian

A DAY IN THE LIFE OF A MIXED MEDIA ARTIST
Emily Mullet

STAY OR GO
Augustine Wong

LYRICS of TRUST TO GROWTH
David Slinger

A DAY IN THE LIFE OF
Ashley West Edwards

GO OR STAY
Terri Fleming

PRAYERS FOR THE WORLD
Ramiro Pianarosa

INSIDE THIS ISSUE

THIS IS

Hello :) It's Lottie here - the person who designs this magazine. We decided to have a different team member introduce each issue to share different aspects of the work that goes into creating this publication. And as you may have guessed.. issue number two is all mine!

As a designer my work starts when the articles have been edited and worked on by talented writers. I get to be the first person outside of the wordsmiths who reads them, so I sometimes act as a sounding board when I start envisioning what layout, graphics and photos would best amplify the piece. I'm also a fine artist who gets to look at artists' creations for hours on end AND call it work!

The uniqueness of each artist already shines through in their pieces but as I'm pairing up artwork with the words from the soul of its maker, that work starts to further blossom on the page. It slowly takes on a new dimension as I move around text, add illustrations, select photographs and push around fonts.

Through the lives of people who create I'm shown that the God of the universe cared enough about us to gift us Creativity. A gift that is, if you purely consider survival and needs, totally unnecessary.

Sometimes we hear of this image of God as a tyrant or a bully who loves holding all our mistakes over our heads. Like, He would look down with his mega tally board where He keeps track of all mistakes

GRACE GO BLOOM NO. 2

and is always looking for unique opportunities to whack you over the head with them.

But it's that gift of creativity that blows that whole image apart. Like repelling magnets, there's no way a tyrant bully like that would give a gift as good as creativity that exists for no other reason to add beauty and meaning to our lives. Because, let's just face it, objectively speaking, art and music and florals and collage aren't necessary for us to make it to the next day. But doesn't creativity just make life wonderfully worthwhile? Creative expression is simply a gift from a Father who wants us to thrive even though there is darkness caused by other people.

I hope we all get the chance to see God as the giver of good things. Good things that move us and give meaning to this life that we've been given. I hope that as you read through this magazine you will pause at each piece of writing, look up its author and the art they create and thank God for their willingness to make this earth more beautiful and meaningful.

Being an artist is a vulnerable undertaking. A piece of ourself goes into each work and is out there for the whole world to see. Throughout this magazine you'll read words of hope and grace and redemption and I hope that you will feel more inspired and bolder in your work. Because if these brave men and women can express themselves and their love for God through their creative practice, so can you.

BEFORE YOU DIG INTO THIS ISSUE, HERE ARE SOME WAYS TO GET STARTED . . .

... take a moment to pause;

... think about how you're feeling right now;

... consider what you're thankful for today;

... prayerfully assess where to grow in your life and your creative practice;

... breath 10 deep, grounding breaths;

... read your Bible as you go;

... grab a pen or highlighters;

... keep notes in the worksheets at the back of this issue starting on page 98.

STORY *by* MARGARET RAMAGE

GOD CAN USE US JUST THE WAY WE ARE

GOD IN HIS ULTIMATE WISDOM AND
CREATIVITY HAS MADE EACH ONE OF US
DIFFERENT. NO TWO OF HIS CHILDREN
ARE EXACTLY THE SAME. AND OUR
DIFFERENCES, OUR QUALITIES AND
TRAITS THAT THE WORLD CAN PERCEIVE
AS WEAKNESS CAN BE TURNED TO
STRENGTHS IF WE PUT OUR LIVES IN HIS
HANDS.

Outsider from the Outset

I grew up in a small Ohio River town in northern Kentucky. Our family was a transplant from the Northeast. Everything about us seemed to set us apart from the culture of the area. My identity through high school was as an outsider. Sweltering summer days, playing around the neighborhood, walking to school and back then, very snowy winters – a wonderful place to grow up, but there was that persistent feeling of belonging somewhere else.

I was the only girl with three older brothers. My mom and dad were good parents. They were loving and provided boundaries that gave me a protected space for imaginary play, reading, writing, and just thinking. There seemed to be plenty of time for just being still. My dad was a diligent worker, a chemist, who took loving care of our house and the yard. He grew a variety of rose bushes and tended a garden. My mom kept our home clean and beautiful. She loved to display teapots and teacups in her family's handmade cabinets. Every summer morning, my dad would bring her roses that she displayed around the house.

A parent's faith

The best gift my parents gave us was the gift of sharing their faith in the Lord. They lived out their faith in a broken world. Mom lived a life framed by childhood trauma and as the Lord encouraged her through my growing up years, she shared the comfort she found in Christ with others in need. When she passed away in July of last year, it was evident her victory in Christ enabled her to forgive all involved in that oppression.

My Dad was her strong emotional and physical support. He still walks daily in the faith in which he grew up, continuing in daily prayer and devotionals at age 96. I am in a place where I can look back and see and taste God's faithfulness in the parents and brothers that He has given me. I get glimpses of the root of God's creativity - how the Lord is re-creating His people through life's struggles and difficulties in a broken world.

"The joy of creating is about the process

A box of pastels

When I was twelve I was given some leftovers of my grandpa's art supplies after his death. At that point, I felt sure I could not draw more than a caricature of a cat and a house. With a box of Grimacer pastels, tracing paper, drawing paper and two art books on trees and faces, I traced and discovered shapes in trees and the colors that made up the cheeks and forehead of a face. I remember re-creating a face from the book that although imperfect, looked back at me in the resemblance of a real person. That was a powerful feeling – using what skills and materials I had in the moment to create an idea that I did not even know that I had.

Grandma's advice

I wish I had listened to my grandma's advice to the adolescent me. She told me not to give up on a creative effort. She was the mentor who taught me to crochet, and she was the encourager who suggested I should finish embroidering that tote bag and not speak unkindly about my drawing on a gift package. If I had only listened to her then, it might have served me well as a young woman to not listen to other's opinions, to get over my need to look good to others and to not be afraid of imperfect creativity; to accept myself with the gifts that I had been given. To live out my life unapologetically using those gifts.

Mentors and friends

Since my mother's passing away last July, it has become more apparent to me that she served as my super mentor. From her I learned to reach out using the areas of my creative interests, home keeping for hospitality and her love for curating beautiful, meaningful family things. A lovely legacy!

I have also been blessed with the friendship of women of faith in my growing up years. Each woman from a different background and in various locations, but willing to encourage me through bible study and sharing common creative interests. Through these friendships I learned to crochet, French hand embroidery, English smocking, to pattern and make children's clothing, scrapbook, collage, watercolor, and acrylic painting.

as much as the finished work."

It has taken me until now to understand that the joy of creating is about the process as much as the finished work. The creativity fostered by family and mentors was just an answering call within me to reflect the Creator in making unique beauty. Each creative finds joy in reflecting parts of our world that God created out of nothing. What an honor and a challenge for me to discover and then pursue different shapes, values and color using bits of paper and paint, shaping them into a botanical or still life. Using these colors and shapes remind me of my early imaginative years when storytelling with my dolls was so effortless – like humming songs without words. They remind me of my dad's roses spread across the house in my mom's favorite vases.

Communicating God's character

I sigh at some of my neuro-differences – I have trouble reading faces and following other nonverbal cues. My reading comprehension of details is the worst. As a non-linear thinker, I can see the big picture and quickly draw conclusions but must work backwards to gather the details. Meanwhile, seeing the big picture and then gathering and gluing many pieces of paper to that makes creating a collage a joy!

I see my art as a continuing means to speak God's word – the truth of Christ's Gospel – intothe time

and place where I live. Gathering my materials, choosing color and content, adapting my choices based on current needs provides an opportunity to be present in expression of the certainty of God's goodness in the moment the paint hits the rice paper, the scissors trim my design, and the acrylic medium spreads across the collage. It is an amazing privilege to find within my week, ways to communicate God's immutable characteristics via spoken and unspoken word.

The heart of truth

One Bible verse that means a lot to me is Nehemiah 8:10

NEHEMIA 8:10 (THE MESSAGE)

"And Nehemiah continued, "Go and celebrate with a

feast of rich foods and sweet drinks, and share gifts

of food with people who have nothing prepared. This

is a sacred day before our Lord. Don't be dejected

and sad, for the joy of the Lord is your strength!"

I am a multi-word, circumlocutory, intuitive type of thinker. This is where scripture helps-cutting to the heart of the truth. My spiritual gift is encouragement. That encouragement encompasses a variety of areas of help. It ranges from physical, concrete ways of serving others to creating vehicles of written and spoken words from His Word to help others. This includes encouragement through creative means as well.

The hard things

I am so proud of my life with my family – my husband and my daughters, sons-in-laws, granddaughter, and grandson. More esoterically, I am proud of accomplishing the hard things – those difficult life adventures that I have cried about because I knew the Lord wanted me to go for it while I preferred a quieter life.

If I could boast, it would be in Christ's work in my life as we leaned on him for adoption, an overseas move, working when I wanted to stay home, starting then walking away from a private practice, trying my first floral collage, and displaying it on Instagram -all concrete actions propelled forward by the Lord with my feet dragging behind with uncertainty.

The big picture

What keeps me going as I face ongoing "disaster" or things not going as planned? I remember that things are going as He planned, and He is good, and I can trust Him. And I am thankful for the support He provides in the patient love of my husband and children.

A crisis in identity

My biggest life changing moment occurred over twenty years ago. I was not getting pregnant when I thought it really was time to do so. We had been married for two years and it was in my timetable to start having the family we wanted. Then we found out there were physical reasons that I might not ever be able to have children. This became a crisis in identity and a crisis of faith. God was not playing out the expected two children and two cat scenario I wanted – pretty much immediately. His answer to our prayer for a child was almost six years of seeming silence. Or was it? During this time, He brought people into our lives to help us face the main thing – His will for our lives as a couple will always come about in His way and in His timing.

Tabletop – Psalm 36:5

Despair to joy

I learned in this long quiet of unexpected waiting that my time is truly in His hands. I needed to recognize His care as we faced surgeries and as He gave us the desire to adopt, through a failed adoption and a long wait for our premature daughter to be brought home. Life changing to become a mother at last but more life changing to meet my Savior in the pit of despair to the joy of holding her for the first time. Christ rescued me from a heart that wanted what I wanted to a heart and soul that desired the life He wanted for me.

Waiting for our daughter to come home to us shaped my motherhood as she eventually became the oldest of our three daughters. I know each child was an unexpected gift from the Lord, not mine to keep but mine to share.

I saw that I could face difficulty and make it through.

He is on my side whether the gift is given or withheld for His own good purpose. It opened my restless heart to His ongoing teaching me of patience. It showed me that my dreams were given me for a reason. That what my heart desired was just a smidgen of what a life lived in Him would look like. It would have been nice to have avoided the difficulties of life. But then who would I be right now without them? I have not faced them alone.

Therapy work

My work life as a speech-language pathologist took root as a growing desire to work in a career that helped society. I landed on speech and language therapy based on my love for literature and language and my growing awareness of my own difficulties in expressing myself verbally. There was an internal understanding of the frustration in effectively communicating thoughts and ideas. That frustration grew into a determined effort to help children with communication disorders. Forty years later, my therapy work continues with children with neurological differences.

My desire to help others joined my need to be creative. It takes imagination and creativity in engaging and sharing attention around what interests the child rather than forcing my own ideas on them. Choosing materials in the moment, making intuitive choices on individual developmental needs in the moment and understanding that each child, made in the image of God, has a desire to communicate verbally or nonverbally their God-given ideas and interests has been a challenge. At the same time it has been a wonderful opportunity that has given me great joy.

I love being present in helping children discover their unique ways to communicate their great thoughts and ideas; enjoying the creative process of engagement and seeing their happiness in being understood by another.

Learning and growing

As I live out my life under the redemptive work of Christ, I have been set free to enjoy exploring creative expression in all areas – all mediums, all substrates. I love learning new ways to use acrylics, watercolor, and gouache in collage work. To this end, I have been taking online classes in those areas with artists who love to use shapes, values, and color as I do. There is a joy to trying new techniques to see how they work. Creativity is an unexpected way into knowing Him better.

Growing into Truth

I am proud of using the gifts God has given me – resting in who I am in Him – imperfect in His already but not yet Kingdom we live in – but growing into that truth because He makes all things beautiful in His time.

I would like to be remembered as a woman who loved the Lord and in living out life as Christ's follower in word and deed. I hope others will see how great a Savior He is. And then understand that the challenge of a life in Christ means that there will be messiness in relationships, selfish words, wrong-headed thinking, and imperfect art. We live in a broken world. And in that brokenness, there is hope.

Maragaret Ramage is an artist and speech-language pathologist. Her desire to help people and be creative have shaped the course of her life, and she has found beautiful ways of using her gifts to point people toward Jesus.

PRAYERS

FOR THE WORLD

JOHN 14:27

PEACE I LEAVE WITH YOU; MY PEACE I GIVE TO YOU.
NOT AS THE WORLD GIVES DO I GIVE TO YOU. LET NOT
YOUR HEARTS BE TROUBLED, NEITHER LET THEM BE AFRAID.

God of all power,

All good things and thoughts come from You.

Ignite in our hearts a real love of peace

And lead the leaders of this world with Your wisdom.

So that Your Kingdom will grow

And move

And spread

Until the earth flows over with the knowledge of Your love

Through Jesus Christ our Lord, Your Son,

Who is alive.

Who rules with You

In unity of the Holy Spirit.

You are One God,

Now and forever.

Amen.

Paraphrased from the

Book of Common Prayer

GROW

Caitlin Forster, a 22 year old artist and student from the Netherlands, has been drawing and painting from a very young age. With a passion for colors and an innate cheerfulness that can't be overlooked, she is finding her way in the world, learning how to infuse her creative gifts into surprising parts of her life.

I live in a small town in the Netherlands. My family home has always had a lovely garden and a warm homey atmosphere where my imagination and creativity was stimulated.

Creativity was passed down to me from both sides of the family. My mom comes from a family of six children and all of them played at least two instruments. All fourteen children in my generation also play an instrument. So we are definitely creative in the sense of music. But even when it comes to drawing and painting, there are seven of us who take it very seriously.

FROM HERE

Diving In

I'm not a very methodical person so there isn't a real process to my work. I always admire the people who make sketches before starting, those who decide on color combinations beforehand. I will often just find a reference picture I like, or several pictures I want to combine. And then I dive in.

I do small sections at a time, then I do some layering. There isn't much rhyme or reason to the way I work. Even though I don't have a specific method of working, I do have some habits that help me. We have a gas stove with a metal top to it. I like putting a cushion on it and getting settled in. It's lovely and warm. All I have to do is turn over the cushion every now and then. It's my favorite place to draw.

Source of Inspiration

My main source of inspiration is Creation. The Lord has made such a masterpiece out of the world that you don't need to look far to find inspiration. No matter what the season is, there is always so much beauty around us. As an artist you're so conscious of what colors you are using, what you want to emphasize. That gives you a different perspective to look at nature, the colors, the shapes.

Visiting new places always fills me with inspiration. When I visit family in South Africa I love painting the scenery and the wildlife.

Another way I gather inspiration is through a file on my phone, which I have labeled "Colors". Whenever I see interesting color combinations that stand out to me I'll take a quick picture and save it there. My grandmother had an old curtain she was getting rid of. The curtain itself was rather ugly, but the colors were gorgeous. It was an unusual combination of lilac and blues and a bit of green. So I took a picture of it and saved it on my phone. And then when I try to find inspiration I will look at my collection of pictures, remember the unexpected color combinations I've come across, and that will help me get started. I love color. I can incorporate that love in my paintings and I try to make things that make me happy.

Confidence Boost

The first time I remember drawing was when I was four years old. My mom was in a meeting at work and I had to wait for her. I was given a large pile of copy paper and enthusiastically worked my way through all of it. I can't imagine it looked very good, but after the meeting all my mom's colleagues were full of praise. It gave me a huge confidence boost and ever since then I've been drawing on everything. Eyes on the corner of a newspaper. Filling in coloring pages with intricate patterns and details. Then I started giving my paintings away and that brought me so much joy. I would give paintings away as teacher's gifts, birthday presents, for any occasion. And people seemed to like it. It encouraged me to keep going.

Medium

My favorite art forms are painting and drawing. I started out drawing when I was very young. I would draw all the time but absolutely hated coloring in. Such a pain. Then I discovered acrylic paints and started painting lots of acrylic paintings. I especially loved painting flowers and birds. When I started high school I discovered water paint and I fell in love with it. I especially love the way the waterpaint is a collaboration between you and the medium. You tell the paint where to go, but it also does what it wants because of the water component. I love that.

I don't like limiting myself to one specific theme or subject. I have always loved painting flowers because they're so pretty. And when you're painting them you can really appreciate how intricate and

Above: Artwork in watercolor by Caitlin.

beautiful and cheerful they are. Everyone likes flowers and birds, so that is something I became very fond of drawing and giving away.

I was always afraid of painting portraits because if it's just a tad off it looks really strange. But I've really grown to love it. I occasionally dip my toe into painting landscapes but I will often still include a person in the field so that I can still convey a certain mood or emotion.

I also love working with air dry clay. I'll make pots, ornaments and fairy houses. Anything quirky that catches my fancy.

Valuable Advice

My high school art teacher gave me some valuable advice. I would always start with the best bits. The eyes, because they were fun. Or the pretty, small details. She would say "Caitlin, don't start with dessert." She'd encourage me to work on the outlines, the less exciting things first. And save the details until the end. I don't always follow her advice, sometimes I will start with dessert. But I remind myself to keep some fun bits for the end. It helps me to keep going and to finish the painting.

Appreciate Your Own Art

I was given another piece of advice by two separate people on two separate occasions. They both told me that it is allowed, it is alright, to appreciate your own art.

When I was young I always felt like I wasn't allowed to be too proud of what I made. Pride is not a good thing but I think it is good to appreciate what you are able to make and how it can make others feel too. If there is something you enjoy doing and the result brings joy to yourself and others, that is a good thing.

One of the people who told me this was so excited about showing me her own art. She would point out details she was proud of, of materials she had enjoyed working with. She'd say things like "Look at this one, it's lovely. Don't you think this one is beautiful?" She was so enthusiastic about her own creations. She liked what she made and she wasn't afraid to say that she liked what she had done with the materials she was using.. That really made an impression on me.

Then I was given the same piece of advice again, from a completely different person. I was visiting a friend in Canada. It was during the time I was deciding whether to go to an art academy or not. We talked a lot about art. She told me not to undervalue myself as an artist. If you undervalue yourself as an artist, other people will do the same.

The Joy of the Lord

I'd like to be remembered as someone who is warm and lets God's light shine. That I treat people around me with respect. That I made other people's day a bit better. I'm reading Anne of Green Gables and there's a nice quote in there "I can just feel that she's glad to be a Christian, and that she'd choose to be one even if she could get to Heaven without it." That really struck me. I want to show the joy of the Lord in that same way.

Weaknesses

One way that God has used my weaknesses for His plan is through my dyslexia. I found school very hard. I still struggle with spelling, with reading and writing. But drawing was always the thing I excelled at. That was the thing I could do, I could get better at. That's probably why I kept going and kept improving. These days I'm fine with my dyslexia because it helps me to connect with people, and it has forced me to learn how to solve problems creatively. It has given me a different outlook on life because I've been problem solving my whole life. It's a skill that is carrying me through my studies right now.

I'm currently studying and working as a remedial teacher in child development and education. I might work in education and help troubled children or children with disabilities, but I will always find ways to mix it with my art. Combining the two, I like using drawings to help my students remember things when they are having a hard time retaining information, is a beautiful way the two intersect and connect.

Glory through failure

I don't like failing so I tend to just keep going. But when I do hit a wall and have to give up, I try to remind myself that God has a plan and that He can be glorified through my failures.

When I had to repeat a year in high school, I felt very sorry for myself. I spent a day wallowing, eating chocolates and being miserable. Then I realized that God is still in control. When I feel like I have failed, it brings a lot of comfort to know that God can do something with my failure.

I know that there is no situation that God isn't in. There is no place where His love can't reach. Even if everything goes wrong, He is still there.

GROWING
PAINS

WORDS *by* ESTHER KARRAM

I DON'T KNOW WHO COINED THE TERM "GROWING PAINS," BUT I THINK THEY WERE BANG ON.

Now, I didn't experience literal growing pains when I was younger – probably because I never actually shot up past five foot, two inches – but I can tell you all about the growing pains of my early twenties.

The pain of a romance switching from declarations of love to a final call goodbye in the span of a week, the pain of fainting spells and visits to the doctor with no answers, the pain of deep heartache and exhaustion as I wondered where God was and why He was allowing things to happen.

But something happened in that pain.

Because of it, I ended up in a counselor's office, finally realizing that I didn't have to do anything to be worthy of love. Because of that pain, I began to realize that my inability to be "100 percent" all the time was not shameful, but okay. Because of that pain, I stopped assuming I knew God's character and opened my Bible to the book of Genesis to ask God to show me who He really was.

Because of that season, I'm different. Stronger. Freer.

But that wouldn't have happened without the pain.

Maybe you're like me and you don't like to embrace pain. Truth be told, I try to avoid it when I can, and I'd rather not walk through painful seasons like my early twenties ever again.

The reality is, though, you and I don't get to pick what moments of pain or difficulty we face. But we do get to choose how we respond to them.

My mom used to have a notecard on our old fridge that was held up by a little heart magnet. I can't tell you where she heard the statement printed neatly on that card or even what the whole thing said, but I remember the first line: "Heather, don't let pain be wasted."

Pain is inevitable – a reality of this fallen world we live in, but you can choose what you do with it.

And I want you to grow from it, friend. As a creative, as a person, as a child of God.

I'm convinced that growth doesn't happen by accident. It takes a series of choices. And while there's no magical path to help you grow in hard times, hopefully these tips point you in the right direction.

#1: Choose to acknowledge your limits

This one brings you face to face with your pride. Pride says, "I'm great at everything" and also "I'm great at nothing."

You are great at what you do, but you're not perfect. There are ways you can improve.

And please know I say this with all the love in the world, friend: You will never grow if you don't first admit what you don't know.

Those who learn are the ones humble enough to say, "I don't know that... and I want to learn."

#2: Choose to lean in.

When hard things happen, your fight, flight or freeze mechanism kicks in. It's how most of us survive.

Can I encourage you though to try something new? Choose to lean in.

Choose in the moment to say, "Okay, where do we go from here?" and "What are the next steps I can take after that flop, that rejection, that set-back?"

This moment has something to teach you. Don't miss it.

And don't be afraid of it.

#3: Choose to ask God what He wants you to learn.

God has something here for you, friend. I don't know what it is, but I know He does.

Ask Him what He wants you to learn and be willing to let Him mold you into His image.

This doesn't mean ignoring your feelings and pretending these growing pains aren't hard. Since God is truth, I believe He delights in our honesty with Him.

I've had yelling and sobbing sessions with God where He has so graciously allowed me to pour out my heartache. And it was only after I poured out that my heart was quiet enough to listen to the truth He wanted to speak over me through His Word and His Spirit.

He wants to hear from you, friend. And He wants to speak. Be willing to pour out and be still.

#4: Choose to keep going, even if it's a direction change.

Don't give up in the hard. Yes, rest is good, but don't claim you're resting when you're looking for an excuse to walk away.

Take what you've learned and are learning and keep moving forward. Maybe you're still moving in the same direction. Maybe this difficulty has shown you that you need to shift your course a little to the left.

That's okay! Directions shift. What matters is that you keep doing what God is calling you to do.

I know growth is hard, friend.

I'm smack in the middle of some growing pains right now and there have been plenty of tears, but I know that I'll look back at this time years down the road and say, *"Wow, you did a lot then, God."*

And He's doing a lot in your life too. He's working in and through you, and His loving hand is with you.

Take heart - there is growth even here.

Esther Karram works as a Creative Manager at a Christian non-profit. She loves writing and is a book enthusiast. Her heart is to paint clear word pictures of the love and hope of Jesus to draw others closer to the heart of God. Esther lives in Ontario, Canada.

WORDS *by* BETSEY IANNARELLI

NURTURING CREATIVITY

There is no better feeling as an artist, than finding yourself in the middle of the creative flow – that place where your ideas, inspiration, and drive to create are just flowing out of you at such a pace that you feel you can hardly keep up. It is an elusive and valuable state of creativity. Sometimes it seems mysterious or like a random occurrence that we cannot prepare for, but here you'll find four practical steps to create an atmosphere for your creativity to flourish. Using the prompts you'll be able to think deeper about your work and the process of creating it.

Recognize the value of your work

As a Christian artist you have probably heard the phrase *"called to create"*. But what does it actually mean?

It doesn't take much looking around to see that the world and everything in it and outside of it was made by a creative God. When we create we echo Him. Your act of creating has the potential to be an act of worship - of bringing glory to God in a way that only you can because you are doing the very thing God created you to do with a heart that is attuned to Him. This truth gives an innate value to your work, and more importantly to the process of creating it. The implications of this are huge! It means that the time and energy we put into our work is worth it regardless of the outcome.

Your work is valuable because when you create you mirror the Creator. Let that truth sink in as you get to work and let it drive you to enjoy the process.

What creative gifts have you been given and how do you see them mirror the Creator?

_____

_____

_____

_____

_____

_____

_____

_____

_____

_____

_____

_____

_____

_____

_____

Make the most of the time you have

While we all may have the urge to set everything aside in order to spend every hour of our day enjoying our craft, doing that will not lead us to a place of creative growth. A quote from Andrew Peterson's book Adorning the Darkness comes to mind, "We may want something harmless but if it's out of place, if it comes before the right thing, then what's benign becomes malignant."

We have already established that your creative work has innate value. Now we need to establish where, in the grander context of all of the responsibilities and blessings in your life, your creative work falls. God blesses a good steward, we can read about this in Matthew 24 in the parable of the talents. When we are good stewards over what God has given us we are both glorifying God and we are helping ourselves create real time and space to create freely.

When I make my own list, most days I am left with one hour or less to devote to my creative practice. I am a mother of two young children who also works outside of the home, and those roles fill the majority of my days. Instead of allowing this meager time to discourage me, I let it inspire me and shape my process.

A few practical things I have done to make the most with the time I have, is to move my current workspace from my studio to my kitchen table. I have also set boundaries on how many pieces I allow myself to work on at one time. In this way I have been able to really make the most of the time I have to create and to enjoy the process itself. But the biggest difference this makes, is that when I sit down to create, I have nothing hanging over my head that I "should be" doing instead. I am relaxed in the knowledge that I took care of the day's tasks and that I can now truly be free to create.

Make a list of your daily priorities and make sure to include your creative work on your list. Be honest about which things need to come first, and remember that if your creative practice is not high on the list it does not mean it is not important. You are making your creative work a priority by intentionally creating time and space to devote to it in the midst of your day.

Shift from product focused to process focused

In this social media obsessed world, having a beautiful finished product to post online and share with the world seems vital. The reality of this can make it hard to enjoy the process of creating. If I am being honest, I have rushed through the process of creating many pieces of art. I have laid out dozens of canvases at one time and worked rapidly on finishing them with the sole purpose of having finished paintings for a photo op. While I might have created something beautiful, I completely missed out on the process in exchange for having a finished piece to show.

Recently I have learned just how much you miss out on when you ignore the process and focus on the outcome. There is real beauty in the actual act of creating something regardless of what the finished product looks like. At the end of the day, you aren't just filling a canvas with paint, or a page with words, or a garden with flowers (or whatever your current art form is!). Your heart and soul are focused on that actual act of creating for that short time whether you acknowledge it or not. I suggest acknowledging it. Not only acknowledging it, but embracing it fully. On focusing on the process, the tools, the space you are working in, on using the gift, talent and creativity given to you by a creative God who finds glory when you are doing the very thing he has made you to do.

I guarantee you will love your finished product even more because you loved the process of making it even more.

Practically, this will look different for everyone. It might look like not sharing your finished product on social media right away. It might look like taking your time setting up your environment until it feels just right, before you start working.

For me, this has been the biggest game changer in my creative practice. A few things I have done are to be intentional and careful about the tools I choose to use, to prioritize fresh flowers to have as nearby inspiration as I paint and as I photograph my work, and to make a cup of tea to help myself slow down. All things to help me enjoy and focus on the process instead of the finished product.

Think back to some of your favorite finished products you have made. What makes those things stick out to you? Write down anything you remember about the actual act of creating that thing. Write down things you can prioritize in your creative practice in order to help you become process focused. Maybe it is new tools that you enjoy using, staying off social media while you work or listening to classical music instead of creative podcasts.

Explore new mediums

In those moments when you feel stuck in a creative rut, one of the best things you can do is to explore other mediums, styles, or subjects. Keep exploring until you find something that clicks. I had this moment myself back in early 2020 when I first began adding embroidery to my paintings. I remember having that "eureka!" moment, where I knew I was on to something exciting because it just fit my interests so well. Since then, when I am experiencing a creative rut I try taking out my oil pastels and devoting time exploring with them. The act of creating something different often opens my mind to new ideas and that excitement often creates an atmosphere for my own creativity to flourish.

Make two separate lists, in one list mediums you would like to try and in the second list subjects you would like to try. When you are feeling stuck come back to these lists and pick one medium and one subject to explore - see what happens!

MEDIUMS:

SUBJECTS:

Our creativity was given to us by God. He gifted us for His glory and for His Kingdom. But that doesn't mean it will always come easy or that there won't be any uphill struggles. Days where we don't know how to move forward. TImes when we feel stagnant. Seasons where we feel stuck.

It is up to us to cultivate the gift we were given. To grow it, nurture it. When we cultivate, we can flourish. When we invest time and energy, we can thrive.

And why do we need to thrive? So that we can better reflect our God, and so that we can glorify Him by giving back from what He has given us.

Betsey is a painter based in PA. You can find her at
www.betseyianstudio.com and instagram.com/betseyianstudio.

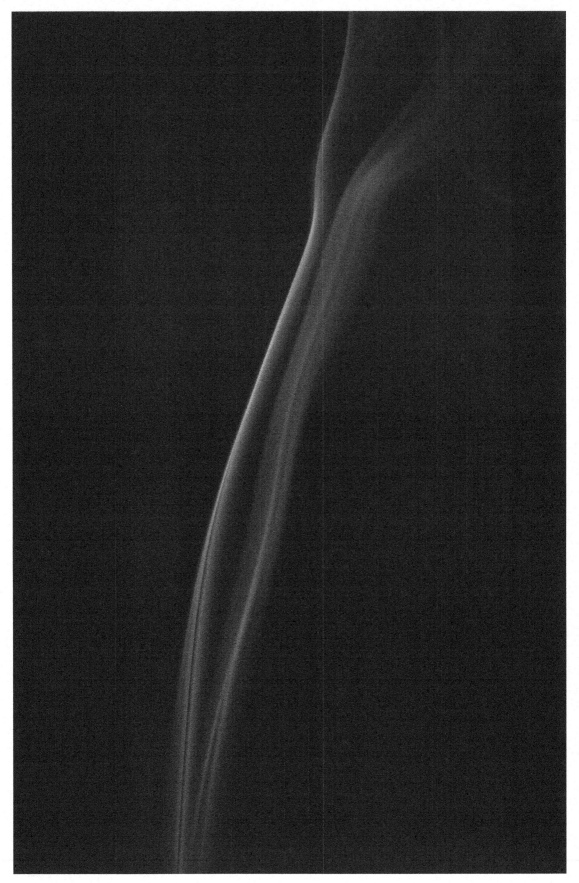

re-fined fire

BY

WORDS *by* MICHELLE PERKETT

God doesn't promise us smooth sailing and easy going when we give our lives to Him. Being a child of God means taking up your cross every day and choosing to follow Jesus, put your trust in Him even when life gets difficult.

But there is also great comfort in knowing that He walks beside us every step of the way and that nothing happens that is not in His control. We can know that, no matter what life throws at us, we can find peace and courage when we look to our Creator for guidance.

I grew up in Burlington, Massachusetts, just north of Boston. As most families in the area, we lived and breathed Boston sports; Red Sox, Patriots, Bruins and Celtics. With three brothers all playing sports, I was immersed in them. But my thing was drawing. My creative encourager was my Dad. He loved singing and music. He would bring home huge pads of perforated computer paper from work and my brothers and I would draw Charlie Brown and Snoopy and other cartoon characters. He always loved to see my drawings and this kept me going towards pursuing a creative path.

At the start

Being a US Air Force veteran, I started my art career as a Graphic Artist in the military. I worked there for four years and then changed direction to corporate Graphic Design before getting my BFA in Illustration. Finally I began pursuing an illustration career. Accomplishing my art degree took a lot of years of intense study, a lot of all-nighters and a lot of bad paintings!

I currently have two businesses, my art and my pet sitting business. I love that I create art that brings me and others closer to Jesus and I love that I get to walk near the ocean everyday. I've been blessed to have wonderful customers in both my businesses over the years.

When troubles come

I had two major life experiences that had a tremendous influence on my art. I was the caregiver for my Mom with Dementia. I also was diagnosed with cancer.

Caregiving for my Mom was the most stressful time in my life. Some days I would come home, pick up a paintbrush and just paint marks and brushstrokes on the pages of my sketchbooks. I had little energy for anything else.

The Lord gave me great strength to care for my Mom and to handle the stress on a daily basis. It was stress that I had never encountered in my life. At the time I also suffered from severe insomnia and every morning I begged for the grace of strength and He always gave me more than I needed.

Consolation

During this time I started a Thirty Day Floral Sketchbook Challenge, just for myself. I drew and painted different florals in watercolor and acrylic.

I found so much peace in it and began adding prayers from the "Litany of Consolation". This way I could go back and read it for encouragement when I needed it the most.

Rise and fall

When my Mom passed in 2018 I was devastated. I had lost not only my best friend, but also my purpose in life. But after a year of intense grieving I slowly developed a line of floral scripture art prints and began selling art again.

The first month of COVID in 2020 I lost ninety percent of my pet sitting business that I had been running since 1998. I was so devastated and blindsighted, it was an extremely heavy cross for me to carry, especially in combination with being isolated during the lockdown. I have dear friends that were there for me during the worst of it and for that I am so grateful. What also kept me going was my art. I needed something to keep my mind occupied so I created a Skillshare class and discovered how much I loved teaching.

Blessings in the broken pieces

Then, in 2021, I was diagnosed with cancer. Having surgery and undergoing chemo treatment was unbelievably difficult. During the treatment I lost almost 30 pounds and was so weak some days I couldn't do most daily tasks. But I have been blessed by having many supportive friends who helped me in so many ways. They prayed for me, encouraged me, and drove me to doctor appointments. They were there on a daily basis to lift my spirits. What kept me going was my faith in Jesus, knowing that He will never leave me or forsake me. Believing that He will give me exactly what I need everyday. I know He was teaching me to deeply trust in Him.

I was so weak I couldn't paint for months. But one day while I was recovering, I painted a mixed media face in my journal and added the words, "There was Jesus." I felt very connected to this song by Zach Williams while I was sick. It gave me so much strength and I never felt alone because I knew Jesus was with me every minute. This painting was my first, "Jesus Girl" as I affectionately call them, that I paint everyday now and they have become my most popular paintings yet!

The turning point

Growing up and for most of my adult life I never felt happy. I was very negative. But meeting Jesus changed all of that. I'm so grateful everyday to Him Who has made all things new in me.

Giving my life to Jesus was the most life-changing experience I have ever had. Until that moment, my life was a life of unhappiness without direction or purpose. I was miserable inside and alway looked at the world and myself so negatively. I truly hated myself and had no self worth. I drank and did drugs and went from one toxic relationship to the next and had all the behaviors of an addict.

But when I met Jesus I was at the point in my life that I was so tired of living my way. I was ready and wanted to obey His way. As I kept saying "yes" to Him I wanted more of Him. I wanted for Him to change me into Himself so I could decrease and He could increase in me. I wanted people to see Him and not me.

Hurting and healing

Since 2011 He has healed me from so many addictions and wounds and has filled my heart with the most indescribable joy that the world could never ever fill. My life has been blessed abundantly by His love. I'm so glad I said yes when He came to find His lost sheep eleven years ago and I pray to always be grateful to Him for setting me free.

Just before I met Jesus I was pretty much at the lowest point in my life. I had just broken up with a person who I let treat me like a doormat, who had no respect for me and made me feel completely worthless.

I was in major credit card debt. At the time I had a rep who sold my first line of art prints and cards at gift shows around the country and I had to buy the floor space for my art and also have it printed which pretty much broke me. On top of that I fell on a dog walk and fractured my knee. Being a full time dog walker at the time I couldn't work which meant I had no income.

A beautiful peace

I truly believe Jesus saw my broken suffering and my tears and had compassion on me. It was like He was saying, "Enough now." And then the miracles came pouring in.

Next spread: Michelle
integrates scripture into
her artwork.

A friend suggested I go to the VA to see if I could get insurance there since I was a veteran. I went and within an hour I was in the ER getting an x-ray. All summer long I had to rest my leg so I spent a lot of time alone. My Mom had given me a St. Jude prayer card and I prayed that prayer over and over for God to help me financially.

Soon after I started attending Mass on Sundays and was invited to go on my first weekend retreat. I cried most of the weekend. The love of God had been poured into my heart for three days straight. I had never felt such a beautiful peace in my life and when I heard the story about Matthew immediately getting up to follow Jesus, I wanted to give Him my yes too.

A few weeks later I was being bombarded by phone calls by credit card companies and couldn't pay my rent. It was so humiliating. I was sobbing on my apartment floor. I had started attending a prayer group and one of the women prayed over me saying, "pray and don't worry about it, just trust Jesus." When I got home I was given the grace of complete calm and trust.

Unexpected help

A couple of weeks later I was ready to do a debt consolidation but I was nervous about being able to pay that balance every month. I spoke to a woman and her husband in my prayer group and told them my plan but they insisted I come to their house for dinner to talk about an alternative to pay off my debt. After dinner they told me they wanted to help me, having been there themselves once and within a few days had paid $20,000 worth of my credit card debt off. I'm still to this day blown away by this gift from the Lord. Again the love of God had been poured into my heart.

I have continued to say yes to Jesus and even told Him to do with me whatever He wants because I knew He would do what is best for me. It has not been an easy journey but along the way I have grown closer to Him and His ways. He has healed me from so many wounds and has slowly been putting my broken life back together and to make me whole. It is such a beautiful life living with Him.

A new life

He has made me realize that I am His beloved daughter who is loved beyond what I could ever imagine and I am worth dying for. He has shown me how to love and how to accept love and has filled my life with so many beautiful things. My favorite thing to do now is to ponder all of His "marvelous deeds" (Psalm 98:1) and His loving care for me everyday. I am so happy I gave Him my yes and I hope I never stop being grateful to Him for changing my life.

When I fell in love with Jesus, He became my greatest mentor. He encouraged me and gave me strength in all areas of my life and built up confidence in myself that I could accomplish anything. I want to become the person God made me to be. I want to be His light in the world, using every gift He gave me to build up His Kingdom.

He is my Strength

One of my favorite scriptures since I've been with the Lord is Philippians 4:13, " I can do all things through Christ who strengthens me." They are words I have prayed and hung onto so many times during the hardest trials of my life; caregiving for my Mom and then grieving her passing, losing my business and not knowing what I was going to do, when I had cancer. He was my strength and carried me through all of it. This verse has been and will always be my hope and strength when I'm afraid and unable to move forward because through Him I really can do all things.

He can make good

Looking back at my life, I would not change anything, either good or bad. God works in all things. He can make good of all my mistakes and failures.

Michelle Perkett is a mixed media artist and art course teacher from California. She is the founder of Michelle Perkett Studio. Find her on Instagram @michelle_perkett, Etsy and Skillshare.

And still,

Given everything in the world

That could go wrong,

Has gone wrong,

And is going wrong,

Here we are,

Making history by overcoming it all.

- Demi Cheryl

GO OR STAY?

Anywhere, any time, God can use you.

MISSIONS ARE DONE FAR FROM HOME. IN DIFFERENT COUNTRIES AND DIFFERENT CULTURES. THROUGH LANGUAGE BARRIERS AND INTO THE GREAT UNKNOWN. THAT'S WHERE *REAL* OUTREACH IS DONE AND WHERE TRUE DIFFERENCE IS MADE. *RIGHT?* OR PERHAPS MISSION WORK IS NOT QUITE SO STRAIGHTFORWARD AS STEREOTYPICAL MISSION WORK IS SOMETIMES SEEN.

Terri Fleming, a retired art teacher based in the US, is using her years of experience and her creative talents to share God's love both in her hometown in Kansas, and at a children's home far away in Southern Africa.

WEEKLY ART CLASSES

Each week Terri teaches art lessons to students ranging from four to seventeen years of age. The families of these students then donate their fees to the children's home in Africa. In this way Terri gives regular support to the sixty children living there at Pasture Valley Children's Home.

These funds have been used, among other things, to purchase a vehicle which has made a *huge* difference to the running of the home and the lives of the children.

PAINTING PARTIES

Besides these art lessons Terri also runs Painting Parties. People host painting parties for their friends. Each friend pays a fee to learn how to paint a scene on canvas. For each party, Terri provides the canvases, paints, brushes, and other materials. She then takes time to teach the group painting techniques. The money raised with these parties are then used to fund Terri's travels to Africa and the work she does there.

VENTURING OUT

From a very young age Terri had a desire to go to Africa, to work with children and to show them God's love. She didn't realize the many years and countless unexpected turns her path would need to take before her dream became a reality and would lead her to Pasture Valley.

Terri shares: "My parents were divorced. My father was an angry alcoholic and my mother a drug addict. We children lived with my mother – usually in poverty. We moved often and lacked electricity, heat, or water service.

Drawing was my refuge from the screaming and violence.

Since kindergarten I loved the safe environment of school. How I was inspired by books, paint, and music. My teachers noticed my desire to help other students, as well as my talent in drawing and painting. Those same teachers encouraged my desire to create, offering me a variety of media and experiences.

At times, I am sorrowful that I cannot show others the love and grace that God has shown me.

My desire is to celebrate His glory through my hands, leading others to Him. God has been so gracious and faithful to me. How I thank Him.

He keeps my focus on Him, His power, and His awesomeness.

God fills me with such joy. For the decades since I have been a Christian, I have been interpreting stories and scriptures in my sketches and paintings. God's promises and Biblical stories inspire me.

My thrill when I read Revelation, Ezekiel, and Daniel create scenes in my imagination. At times, it takes months to interpret the glory and to determine how to express the thrill on canvas."

CHILDREN'S HOME

When Terri visits the children's home she helps out at the primary school and also teaches art classes. Many of the children grew up without any exposure to creativity, to the joy of dreaming things up and making them come to life. Terri loves teaching them new skills and techniques to help them express themselves and grow.

RAISING FUNDS

Now, because of looming civil unrest and the ever-changing covid regulations, Terri has not been able to visit Pasture Valley for quite some time. But that does not mean her mission has been put on hold. She might not be able to go abroad but she is still working hard and finding ways to make a difference.

Terri continues to use her painting skills to raise funds and awareness for the children that have become so dear to her.

SERVE THE PEOPLE YOU MEET

God can use us wherever we are. You might get called to step out into the world. To be part of something exciting and out of the ordinary. But maybe you are one of the ones called to stay. Maybe your mission is to look around your neighborhood and community for opportunities to serve God and to serve the people you meet. And that is important in its own extraordinarily ordinary way.

AS EACH HAS RECEIVED A GIFT, USE IT TO SERVE ONE ANOTHER, AS GOOD STEWARDS OF GOD'S VARIED GRACE.

1 PETER 4:10 (ESV)

REFLECT

1 WHAT IMPACT HAS YOUR BACKGROUND HAD ON YOUR ART? DID IT HELP OR HINDER YOUR CREATIVITY?

2 ARE YOUR CREATIVITY AND YOUR FAITH INTERTWINED OR ARE THEY TWO SEPARATE ASPECTS OF YOUR LIFE? IS THIS A GOOD THING?

3 HAVE YOU EVER FELT GOD ASK YOU TO USE YOUR CREATIVE SKILLS FOR HIM? IN WHAT WAY?

4 WHAT WOULD IT LOOK LIKE FOR YOU TO PUT GOD AT THE CENTRE OF YOUR CREATIVITY?

5 WHAT IS A NEW WAY YOU CAN USE YOUR GOD-GIVEN SKILLS FOR HIM?

DAY IN THE LIFE OF A

MIXED MEDIA ARTIST

WORDS BY EMILY MULLET

Previous spread: Work in progress for
an art project of Emily's.

Right and next page: 'Luella', an
art piece in Emily's Mind Blooms
collection.

IT SOUNDS FUNNY to say this, but I've had a hard time allowing myself to do what I find the most fun, which is making art! If I'm enjoying my labor, it feels like I'm doing something wrong. Crazy, right?

When I first quit my day job in August of 2021, I found it much easier to pour myself into my magazine and online community. I even put house projects above my art making because I felt so uncomfortable about it!

Even though I had carefully planned and made the choice to become a full time artist, it was really difficult to justify spending my days making art. What helped me get past this was first recognizing my behavior and then unraveling why I was making these choices. Not to mention, when I actually looked at the numbers, the majority of my income was from my fine art sales. Turns out you can have fun and make money at the same time. Who knew?!

A DEDICATED STUDIO SPACE

When we were house hunting, one of my top criteria was to have a room dedicated to studio space. I am fortunate to have a studio in my home that I can fill with whatever art supplies and creations I desire. Another reason why we purchased this specific property was for the detached three car garage out back. We are in the midst of converting it into a gallery space where I can host my own art shows and events.

Making the decision to go full time was absolute torture! In December of 2019, I realized I had been at my day job for over seven years. That fact completely caught me off guard.

I realized I had intentionally held myself back from my full potential as an artist and a human in general. I had completely ignored who God designed me to be and invested in a safer version myself. This realization filled me with an absolute fire to make up for lost time.

GROWING LIKE NOBODY'S BUSINESS

Entering 2020, my goal was to make so much art that by the end of the year I would be embarrassed of what I had made at the beginning of the year. I wanted to grow like nobody's business. Fortunately that goal paired well with the unexpected pandemic. I was up before work making art until I had to hop online. As soon as five o' clock hit, I would shut my computer down and race back to my studio and work into the night. Weekends were like a glorious art retreat for me. I would be holed up in my studio working nonstop.

A NATURAL RHYTHM

I documented much of this personal experience through Instagram. With the entire world on lockdown, there was an eager audience to consume my story. My goal wasn't to sell

the work, I simply wanted to grow. But after several inquiries to purchase my art, I figured it would be simpler to set up a website to cut down on the back and forth messaging. To my surprise, as soon as I listed the work, it started selling. A natural rhythm developed where I would work feverishly on a collection, launch it, and sell it. After a year of this steady cadence, I began to think I might actually be able to be a full time artist.

HELLO, CONVICTION

That spark of hope wasn't enough to convince me though. The thought of an inconsistent paycheck was terrifying. Also I was proud of working successfully in a creative industry where I managed large projects and could multitask like a champ. However, I knew deep down, it was time to move on even if it wasn't to become a full time artist. I prayed SO much about my decision. I constantly begged God for wisdom and discernment. During this time I was reminded of the Old Testament story of Jonah, and how everyone on the ship suffered with him because he would not go where God had called him. Hello, conviction. It was time to make a plan to become a full time artist. My husband and I created several financial goals to reduce our monthly expenses. Once we hit those, I put in my two weeks notice. I am beyond thankful that I can say with full honesty, I do not regret my decision at all.

MORNING ROUTINE

When I became a full time artist, one of the biggest changes I had to make was focusing my mind to a healthy place, creatively and spiritually, at the start of my day. To maintain this practice, before going to bed, I make sure I have three books placed on my nightstand. The first is a poetry book by Tess Guinery (I alternate between The Apricot Memoirs and The Moonflower Monologues). When I wake up (after a little scroll through instagram), I read a couple poems to kick off my morning mindset. After that,

I'll go through a devotional, typically from She Reads Truth, and then spend some time in prayer. Finally, I open my planner and write down the top 3-5 things I want to accomplish that day.

VARIETY OF ROLES

After my morning routine, my days vary depending on what deadlines I have coming up, or meetings I have on the calendar. If I'm meeting with other artists, I try to schedule them early in the morning so it doesn't cut too much into my workday. My work is divided into several categories. My primary focus is making art. I also have an art magazine and online community that documents and amplifies local artists in my town *(Editor's Note: artistsofpxv.com)*. I provide social media content assistance for artists and creatives, and most recently, I've stepped into the online teaching space. As you can imagine, there are lots of different goals and priorities I'm constantly bouncing between.

Between these various roles, one thing that keeps me creating personal work is my commitment to a weekly vlog that goes out to my email list every Friday. From sketching, to screen printing, concrete sculpture, and even stop motion video experiments, the vlog documents whatever I am creating that week. Not only does it keep me accountable to my creative practice, it has become a way to form a deeper connection with my audience. I am very comfortable with bringing my followers on my creative journey. I let them experience my high moments of discovery as well as messy failures.

GOING WITH THE FLOW

Aside from scheduled meetings, I am very intentional to go with the flow as my day unfolds. As I mentioned before, I write my top goals for the day so I mostly stay on track. If something is not working in the studio, or I'm really in the zone on a particular project, I allow myself to pivot and adjust as needed. I've found staying in tune with myself in this way is the most effective method of working.

A DAY IN THE LIFE OF ARTIST EMILY MULLET

morning

01. read poetry for the morning mindset

02. go through deviotional

03. pray

04. plan out top 3-5 things for the day

afternoon

-- make art

-- meetings

-- work on art magazine

-- social media content assistance for artists

-- teaching

-- weekly vlog

-- email list

-- share my creative journey

WORDS OF ADVICE

My constant advice to fellow artists when they don't know what to do, or they feel like they are on the wrong path, is this: Do the thing that they are most excited about, and also the thing that is the easiest for them. Finding that flow state is an incredibly effective way to work.

Emily Mullet, a mixed media artist based in Phoenixville, PA, has a diverse background ranging from ceramics to painting. In her current mixed media work, Emily collages screen printed florals to create portraits of women. The portraits symbolize what it looks like to tend the garden of your own mind. The figures depicted have chosen to care for their native plants, instead of forcing non native plants to grow.

By prioritizing natural gifts and interests, the garden of the mind naturally becomes more complex and beautiful than anything planned. Emily received a Bachelor of Arts in studio art with an emphasis in painting and graphic design from the College of the Ozarks in 2012.

CONNECT WITH EMILY at www.emilymullet.com & Instagram: @emilymullet.

WE ALL HAVE A STORY.

We all walk, learn, grow, struggle, and persevere. You. Me. All of us. You can use your story to reach out and touch another person trying to walk their own path.

For our upcoming issues we are looking for Christian creatives who are willing to open up about their life, their art and the role God has played in it. You get to write your story or we'll help you do so. We always check with writers before going into print for final approval.

If you are interested in being interviewed or to write for an upcoming issue of Grace Go Bloom, please email Eleanor at editor@gracegobloom.com and give us a quick intro into who you are and what you do.

DEVOTIONAL

by JESSICA RUPP

We can very much have a love/dislike relationship with growth. Sometimes growth feels like a field of wildflowers– blooming with new things sprouting up into a lovely existence.

Sunny days with perfect temperatures all the time. In this space we fall in line with every part of who we are. We find ourselves thinking 'I love growth, look at how far I have come.'

But let's be real about the other seventy five percent of how we feel about growth. Growth can be painful. It can be like grabbing a rose and the thorns grab you back. It can be like a bandaid that gets pulled off and it feels like it took all your skin with it. Or like a war trench and you're just trying to catch your breath before the next gun goes off.

It can look scary and have many unknowns. It can be a space where lies start to creep up and flood your mind. "I can't do this Lord, it will hurt and I am not strong enough. Is there a break, because I am tired... I can't breathe and need to rest. The enemy is winning, why do I feel like I am just losing?"

Isn't it interesting, sitting in a place where we fear growth because we are used to living in pain or failure? We allow ourselves to believe it is better to live in our past than it would be to choose to step into something new. We become scared of the unknown that growth brings along with it.

We crave a safe place to enter the garden of our souls and to watch growth happen. Don't get me wrong, a safe place to grow is always lovely, but sometimes our growth needs to happen in the trenches of our soul.

The Father, in His kindness, desires to see us grow. His uncontainable passion to see us walk in more unity with Him, means that He cannot sit by and watch us stay stagnant in our sins. He calls us up. He calls us to a place where we get to choose.

We can choose to sit in what we think is good for us, or we can decide to take a step into growth, into becoming more like Him. He created the garden of our Spirit to be a place of rest, where we see growth, where we celebrate it and water it. He holds us as we walk through the trenches of our garden.

I have had a peace lily plant in my kitchen for four years. Two years ago it stopped producing any blooms. It has slowly grown and yet I have had to cut back dead pieces for the last two years. I really did not think it would make it. Then one day, I walked in my kitchen after years of not seeing any blooms and something caught my eye. There is a small bloom. I saw the white bloom starting to open up. It brought me to the inner garden where growth has felt hard the last two years. The Father in His gentle voice said, "Peace has been awakened, growth has taken place and now step into the beauty of what is to come. Do not give up my child, for I see you, and I honor you. All of Heaven cheers you on. Now allow growth to sprout up a bloom and thrive."

Growth is hard, but out of the kindness of our God, He says we will not be alone. He is with us. Maybe we need to venture into the garden of our soul and clean it up. A gardener never just walks away from his garden and says 'okay, I am done'. He spends time taking care of it, watering it, planting new things to breathe more life into it. He pulls up the weeds and even takes out the plants that are no longer alive.

May we enter into this space without fear or give power to lies that say 'we can't do it.' Growth can be a place where we can breathe again and then breathe it onto others.

Sap Green is soft and at the same time full of depth. It breathes growth and renewal. Succulents are full of sap green. This color can even take on other colors to alter its beauty to something that is breathtaking. The growth of a succulent can be slow and ever so steadfast. It is resilient.

The Father invites us into growth with him. The garden of our soul is a place where the Holy Spirit loves to be, where God breathes life into something new and a place where Jesus loves to abide. The Trinity does not expect it to happen overnight.

Growth takes time, taking care of a garden takes time. The Father is not disappointed when we mess up. He just asks that we keep moving forward.

pray & read

ISAIAH 58:11

_____

_____

_____

_____

_____

_____

_____

_____

PROVERBS 28: 19-28

_____

_____

_____

_____

_____

_____

_____

_____

"A garden enclosed is my sister, my spouse; a spring shut up, a fountain sealed."

SONGS 4:12

reflect

**FIND SPACE WHERE GROWTH CAN HAPPEN. LET YOURSELF SEE HOW FAR
YOU HAVE COME, EVEN IF IT'S ONLY FOR A SHORT MOMENT EVERY DAY.**

_____

_____

_____

_____

_____

_____

**ALLOW GROWTH TO TAKE UP ROOM IN MY SPIRIT SO MY SOUL AND
BODY CAN BREATHE AGAIN.**

_____

_____

_____

_____

_____

_____

THE INNER GARDEN OF MY SOUL CAN THRIVE WHEN I PUT THE TIME INTO IT.

_____

_____

_____

_____

_____

_____

MY GOD IS A GOOD GARDENER, HE PRUNES, HE WATERS, HE SPEAKS LOVE, HE CREATES NEW THINGS WHERE GROWTH IS TAKING PLACE.

_____

_____

_____

_____

_____

_____

"FOR WE ARE CO-WORKERS IN GOD'S SERVICE; YOU ARE GOD'S FIELD, GOD'S BUILDING."

1 Corinthians 3:9

COLOR
LOVERS

Color Devotionals for artists

52 devotions
around colors

COMING 2022/2023

BIG NEWS!

If you've enjoyed the color devotionals by Jessica, you'll be pleased to learn that Grace Go Bloom is publishing a full color book filled with color theory, meditations, scripture and color mixing recipes. Be sure to sign up at gracegobloom.com to get notifications of new publications such as this one.

THERE'S ALWAYS A RISE
WHEN THE SUN'S INVOLVED

& THERE'S ALWAYS
A FALL IN THE DARK

& WHILE THE STEPS THAT YOU'RE SEEING
MIGHT LOOK LIKE AN END

LET THESE WORDS
CARRY YOU ON

CAUSE SOMEDAY YOU'LL BE *BACK HOME.*

RISE, MY CHILD, *I MADE YOU TO GROW*
AND *FIGHT THIS FIGHT*

David Slinger is a singer/songwriter from Cape Town, South Africa. His latest release is the EP "It's all about Hymn". Follow him on Instagram via @david_slinger_music

REFLECT & GROW

Throughout this issue you've read about growth from different perspectives. As this issue comes to a close, use some of these prompts and exercises to unpack where you want to spiritually, artistically and personally grow next.

What is a truth about God that you learned or were reminded of in this issue? What does this mean to you?

_____

_____

_____

_____

_____

_____

_____

_____

_____

_____

_____

_____

_____

_____

_____

_____

_____

_____

_____

_____

_____

What is something you are afraid to accomplish? Where does that fear come from?

What are some positive changes you have made since the beginning of this year?

List 5 10 things you have accomplished.

1. _____

   _____

2. _____

   _____

3. _____

   _____

4. _____

   _____

5. _____

   _____

6. _____

   _____

7. _____

   _____

8. _____

   _____

9. _____

   _____

10. _____

    _____

What are some habits in your life you need to change?

_____

_____

_____

_____

_____

_____

_____

_____

_____

_____

_____

_____

_____

_____

_____

_____

_____

_____

_____

_____

_____

What are some good habits you would like to start?

What are some changes you would like to see in your life in five years?

What steps are you going to take to accomplish these changes?

1. _____

_____

2. _____

_____

3. _____

_____

4. _____

_____

5 _____

_____

6. _____

_____

7. _____

_____

8. _____

_____

9. _____

_____

10. _____

_____

Write a prayer asking God to show you areas where you need to grow, and committing to taking the necessary steps.

_____

_____

_____

_____

_____

_____

_____

_____

_____

_____

_____

_____

_____

_____

_____

_____

_____

_____

_____

_____

_____

NOTE FROM
THE EDITOR

I loved putting together this issue of Grace Go Bloom.

The thing that stood out to me most about this issue was how almost every article, every in-depth profile and every personal story ended with roughly the same conclusion: Yes, life has thrown me some curveballs, there have been struggles and difficulties along the way. But it has grown me into the person I am. It has cultivated my relationship with the Lord. And looking back, I wouldn't have it any other way.

Isn't that just so encouraging?

God never promised us that there wouldn't be any troubles on the road. We know from Scripture that we are not guaranteed an easy, hassle-free life. But we are promised God's presence through every valley and every tough season. We can know that we are not walking the road alone.

A few years ago I felt unsatisfied in my life and my ministry working for a children's home in Swaziland. I felt like I was mediocre at many things, not particularly good at anything and I felt fear about taking on new challenges. I compared myself to my friend Alicia, someone I deeply admire. She lives her life without fear. Leave the US and move to Africa? Sure! Run a care center for vulnerable and abused girls? Yes! Start a preschool in a disadvantaged area that helps kids get a headstart AND hear the Gospel? Why not!

And I realized the big difference between us was that when opportunities arise, she prays about it and if she feels God is asking her to take on a project, she trusts that He will guide her every step of the way. She feels comfortable not knowing what the end result will be, because she knows that that is in God's hands. But when any new project came my way, I would think of all the reasons why I would not be able to do it.

So I have tried to bring a bit of Alicia into my attitude to life. I consider new projects, and assume that if it is a good project that I feel God wants me to do, He will help me with it..

Every day I enjoy the growth I see in my capabilities, my confidence and my faith in God. I now teach classes I never thought I would be able to teach. I am looking forward to going back to school. I take on new projects and challenges and enjoy the learning process. And every day I rely on God to walk me through it all.

Of course this doesn't mean everything I do is a success. Not even close! But we are not made to be stagnant. We press on, we strain forward and we keep our eyes on Jesus, because He is there every step of the way.

Philippians 3:12-14

[12] Not that I have already obtained this or am already perfect, but I press on to make it my own, because Christ Jesus has made me his own. [13] Brothers, I do not consider that I have made it my own. But one thing I do: forgetting what lies behind and straining forward to what lies ahead, [14] I press on toward the goal for the prize of the upward call of God in Christ Jesus.

Yours in Christ,

- Eleanor

grace go bloom
PRINT MAGAZINE

THANK YOU for supporting us by purchasing this issue. If you have questions or to submit an idea for our next issue please contact us through email *editor@gracegobloom.com* or through our website *gracegobloom.com*.

WANT TO HELP? As a small team we hope you could pray for us for vision, ideas and guidance in all things. It would also mean a lot to us if you shared about this magazine with friends and your church community so we can create more opportunities for artists.

WRITE OR CREATE WITH US? Find submission guidelines & opportunities for submitting artwork or lyrics on *gracegobloom.com*

www.gracegobloom.com
@gracegobloom

Made in the USA
Las Vegas, NV
04 August 2022